The Colors of Grace in Our Homes

by
Stuart Tyner

Advent*Source*

The Colors of Grace in Our Homes

Series Coordination: John Hancock Center for Youth Ministry
Series Editor: Stuart Tyner
Book Design: Stuart Tyner
Cover Design: Wendy Miller / V. Bailey Gillespie
Copy Editor: Sharon Churches, Joyce Jesse

ISBN 1-57756-001-9

The Colors of Grace in Our Homes

Contents

Dedication

To parents, teachers, pastors, lay leaders, youth, and children
who aim at making the grace of Jesus Christ
central in their homes

Introduction

by V. Bailey Gillespie and Stuart Tyner

"When I found out about how the youth of the church felt about the caring climate of our home, I knew that my instincts were correct. I have felt all along that we needed to spend more quality time together sharing our feelings about God and His guidance in our lives."

"I had no idea that stressing the negative prohibitions of our Christian lifestyle made youth feel so alienated from the church. I am going to spend time through family discussions talking about positive Christian life, because I know it has a more positive impact."

"When I think of the things that have made my spiritual life rich, I remember times when as a family we tried to care for someone in need, and when we raised money to help another church overseas. I am going to try to teach my children the importance of service and caring."

Translating theological truths, statistics, and philosophical understanding into practical Christian applications may be one of the most complex tasks that religious people are ever asked to do.

Practical Counsel from King David

David, the Shepherd King said, "Come, my sons, listen to me, I will teach you the fear of Yahweh. Which of you wants to live to the full, who loves long life and enjoyment of prosperity?" (Psalm 34:11, 12)

We all want that kind of fulfillment.

In answer to his question, rather than giving theological explanations, David provides practical counsel. He says, "malice must be banished from your tongue, deceitful conversations from your lips; never yield to evil, practice good, seek peace, pursue it." (Psalm 34:13, 14)

We are always tempted to give more information to others in the belief that all of this knowledge will somehow change them. And while it is clear that good theology is always crucial if the practice of Christianity is to be focused, what people often need most is the "how to" of Christianity.

Valuegenesis Research

When the massive research project called *Valuegenesis* was com-
pleted by the Search Institute staff in Minneapolis and evaluated by the committee of scholars who developed the questionnaires about faith, values, and commitment, it was immediately recognizable that the massive amount of data would only be helpful if it could be put to use.

We need to be practical.

A Focus on Loving Christians

This has been the center of our prayers ever since.

• We hoped people might change to become more open, loving Christians.

• We wondered if Christian homes might become more able to communicate about things of importance in the Christian life.

• We wanted to understand how to be more victorious and happy.

• And most importantly, we realized we needed to understand the implications of the statistics about grace, and love.

This is especially true of our homes, religious schools, and congregations.

That is what implementing *Valuegenesis* is all about.

The Importance of the Family

We know that the family is the crucial laboratory in which the faith and values of our children are developed. *Five things have become important due to the research about faith, values and commitment.* If we could begin to implement these suggestions, we might see changes begin to happen.

Mother: When the mother is highly religious, is comfortable talking about her faith, shares her faith often with her children, and has discussions about faith with the young people, youth are more likely to mature in faith and develop commitment to a religious outlook.

Father: When the father is highly religious, is comfortable talking about his own faith, often shares his faith with his children, and has regular discussions about faith with them, they are more likely to reveal a growing mature faith and a sense of loyalty to their denomination.

Support: When parent-child communication is frequent and positive, when family life is experienced as loving, caring, and supportive, and when parents frequently help their children with school work, youth are more likely to possess a growing, rich faith, and a sense of loyalty to their denomination.

Control: When parents hold strong standards, and enforce them fairly, firmly, and lovingly, punish wrong behavior, and set limits on their child's use of time, the young people tend to grow in mature faith and manifest commitment and loyalty to their church. Though control factors have the least impact of any of the five groups, control seems to be positive for the home environment even though it is not for the religious school and the congregation. When discipline comes from people whom we know love us, it is best received.

Spiritual togetherness: When the family frequently engages in worship together, and that worship is interesting and meaningful, and when the family engages in projects to help other people, the children and youth are more likely to manifest a growing, rich, mature faith and loyalty to their denomination.[1]

In Need of Spiritual Growth

Now that we understand the primary dynamics of the family's contribution to faith maturity and loyalty to the church, we can put this understanding into practice as we approach the spiritual areas in which our families are in desperate need of growth. *Valuegenesis* revealed four such growth areas:

• Establishing a grace orientation in which we experience the peace that comes from accepting the saving love of God. Such an orientation stands in sharp contrast to a behavior orientation in which we experience the condemnation that comes from representations of a critical God.

• Fostering a faith maturity in which we discover the joy of worshipping God in every aspect of our lives. This maturity does not come through the endorsement of a *segmented* spirituality in which we limit our worship of God only to religious aspects of our lives.

• Creating a faith development climate in which we experience the acceptance and openness of, and the active involvement in an inclusive community of faith. Unfortunately, far too many of us grow up in a segregated community in which we experience the loneliness and frustration of, and the ultimate alienation from a community which does not include us.

• Providing service opportunities through which we implement a consistent commitment to minister to the needs of others. Such a dynamic is radically different from a content-only focus in which we ascertain information, but are not encouraged to put our faith into action.

Four Dynamics for Spiritual Growth

These four dynamics form the outline of this book. In each of the chapters about grace, worship, community and service you'll discover 25 easy-to-understand, easy-to-implement activities to do alone or with the other members of your family. It's our prayer that these 100 practical recommendations are just the beginning of an exciting journey your family takes exploring the incredible, rich grace of God.

[1] Roger L. Dudley, with V. Bailey Gillespie, *Valuegenesis: Faith in the Balance* (Riverside, CA: La Sierra University Press, 1992), 202-203.

Establishing a Grace Orientation

The Parable of the Welcoming Father

Assign characters from the parable in Luke 15:11-32. You'll need a father, two sons, and a servant, so if your family's small, you may have to assign more than one part per person.

Read the parable in the Bible, then act out the parable, only don't use any words; exaggerate all the actions. Before you begin, think about how you'll portray each emotion. Practice being arrogant, demanding, extravagant, remorseful, gracious, joyful, resentful, and full of wisdom.

When you've finished your production, reflect on what Jesus is trying to teach us in the parable. You may want to add these questions to your discussion: Who's the hero of the story? Why do we usually call this story the parable of the prodigal son? Is there a better title? What did the son have to do to *earn* the father's forgiveness? Where did the father look for his son? What do the actions of the father teach us about God's grace?

Seeing Grace in the Faces of Our Friends

What evidences of grace have you experienced in the lives of people you have known? Have there been a couple of instances in which someone exemplified grace to you through their actions?

Think about an example of grace in the lives of your friends or family members. Share that experience with your family.

Free, with No Strings Attached

When God tells us that His grace is free (see Ephesians 1:6 and Romans 3:24, for example), does He really mean free? Or are there strings attached?

Or is the problem that we don't always use the word "free" correctly?

Get together a couple of weeks of newspaper ads and coupons (the ones in the Sunday paper are good). Cut out coupons and ads that offer something for free, but in the fine print explains that the offer is really not free ("with the purchase of . . ." or "for six box tops . . .").

Explain what free means.

In Him We *Have* Forgiveness

One of the most significant and personal aspects of God's grace is His forgiveness of our sins, full and free and final. Read Ephesians 1:7 and 8.

Discuss forgiveness. How do you feel when you've been forgiven? How difficult is it for you to forgive others? What forgiveness experience has been most meaningful to you?

Examples of Grace from Planet Earth

Let's try to understand God's grace more completely by comparing it to earthly systems we understand a little bit better.

Choose one of the illustrations from the column to the right and quickly talk about everything you know about the subject. Then reflect on what you've discussed. What's the same and what's different between this human system and God's economy of grace?

a. **Adoption**. Talk about orphans, birth certificates, foster homes, adoption papers, etc.

b. **Today's legal system**. Talk about crime, arrest, trial, defense and prosecution, sentencing, punishment, parole, etc.

c. **The medical profession**. Talk about disease or injury, admission to a hospital, emergency treatment, physicians and nurses, cure, etc.

d. **War and peace**. Talk about what starts a war, about casualties, battles, conditions for peace, etc.

Gift Wrapped with Lots of Love

We often refer to grace as a gift from God. Giving and receiving a gift can provide a stimulating start to an exciting discussion about grace.

Save a little money and buy a gift for someone special (a brother or sister, Mom or Dad, classmate or teacher, etc.). Make it a surprise, not a birthday present or a gift connected with any holiday.

Express how you felt giving the gift. What would have caused the recipient to refuse the gift? Why do we so often ask, "What did I do to deserve this?" What does this activity teach you about God's gift of grace?

The Color of Grace in Our Everyday Lives

C. S. Lewis once remarked that he believed in Christianity as he believed in the sun; "...not only because I see it, but, by it I see everything else."[1]

In the same way, God's grace should color our entire day, everything we experience, and all our relationships.

Get a box of crayons or colored pens and a piece of blank white paper for each member of your family.

Choose one color that best represents grace to you. Then draw a picture that portrays one aspect of your everyday life. Use only the color you've chosen.

Analyze your picture. Explain the reason you chose your color and describe the scene you've drawn. How does God's grace impact ev-

Talking to God without Being Afraid

In the Bible there are a number of stories about imperfect people being consumed by God's presence. (See, for example, the story of Nadab and Abihu in Leviticus 10; and the story about the Philistines who looked at the ark in 1 Samuel 16. Also read about Moses' fear in Exodus 3:6.) Even the appearance of angels causes fear in humans. (See the words of encouragement to Joseph in Matthew 1, to Mary in Luke 1, and to the shepherds in Luke 2.)

Think about a time when you felt you were in God's presence, but you weren't afraid of God. Remember, every time you pray, you enter God's presence. Every time you go to church you invite God's presence to be with you.

How can we sinful humans be unafraid in the presence of a perfect God? Read Romans 5:1-10 and 1 John 4:15-18 and come to some conclusions about how God's grace destroys our fear.

What Did I Do
to Deserve This?

Think about all the things we do in this world to earn rewards or favor. Have you done all your chores? Did you finish your homework? Did you do a good job? Are you working on the skills for being a good friend? If you work hard enough, your boss will give you a raise.

What are some of the other areas of our lives where we have to work for our rewards?

Compare the way we work for a living with the way God gives us His grace. (See Romans 6:23 and Ephesians 2:8.)

The Mission's Powerful
Picture of Grace

Rent a copy of the 1986 film, *The Mission*. In this true story about South American missionaries, Robert De Niro plays a mercenary named Mendoza who has killed and enslaved natives and murdered his own brother in a fit of jealousy. The first part of the film portrays the brutality and deepening wickedness of this character.

Then, in despair, Mendoza declares that there is no salvation for him, no penance difficult enough. But a priest, Gabriel, devises a penance: climbing to the top of a huge waterfall to the same village where Mendoza has terrorized the natives.

In 11 minutes of stunning emotion, the film shows how hard we try to atone for our own sins and how utterly futile such attempts are.

The conclusion of the scene, in which we see forgiveness in its most pure and joyous expression, is a spiritual experience you'll never forget. One pastor, after viewing this scene, remarked, "I've never understood grace more clearly."

Preview the first part of the film to decide how much you want your family to see. Then watch the film together, stopping at the conclusion of the scene to explore the power and beauty of grace.

Singing Hymns About Grace

Search through the hymnal to find songs that include the word "grace." Sing the songs together. Stop to discuss the words of the hymn. What can you relate to in the song?

What would you like to say about grace if you were writing a song? Compose a verse to match the music of one of the hymns you've discovered.

Paul Writes to the People at Your House

Collect a number of New Testament versions and open to Ephesians, chapter 2. Read verses 4-10 in the different versions. Listen to Paul's words of counsel to the people at Ephesus.

Now take the time to *personalize* these verses so they become Paul's words to the people at your house.

Replace the words, "we," "us," and "you," with your name. Then put the personalized verses in a place where you'll see it every morning when you wake up. You may even want to memorize the verses and recite your version at another worship time.

Getting Even in a Positive Way

Do something nice for someone who has recently been unkind to you. Don't make any reference to the unkindness. Just exchange pleasantness for meanness.

That's a pretty difficult assign-ment, isn't it? Why do you think it's so hard to do? Do you think it's easier or more difficult for God to forgive us and give us His love? How is your action the same as God's? How is it different?

Earning Our Salvation

The Bible is clear that there is nothing we can do to *earn* our salvation. (See Romans 3:20.) Let's agree that *nothing* really means *nothing*.

Then consider the religious things we do: going to church every week, faithfully giving our offerings, reading our Bibles every day, and working for others. And how about the things we do at home, like obeying our parents, keeping our rooms clean, washing the dishes without complaining, and getting ready for the Sabbath?

If we can't do anything to earn our salvation, what is the reason we do the good things we do? How can we better distinguish between the good works Christians do and God's grace, the basis for our salvation?

A Perfect Clay Pot Gets Broken

Let's look at the concept of being perfect.

Buy a clay pot at a garden supply store, the type of pot in which you'd plant small flowers. Look carefully at the pot. There are no cracks or breaks in it. You could say it was in perfect condition.

Now take a hammer and lightly break a section of the pot. Try not to smash it to pieces! Just break off a little bit. Give everyone in the family a whack at the pot. Each of those breaks is like what happens in our lives when we sin.

Next, try to glue the pieces of the pot back together. You'll be able to do a fairly good job of reconstructing it. But when you're all through, how perfect is the pot now? Even if the pot is never broken again and it becomes quite useful, is it ever going to be perfect again? What chance does this little pot have of getting into a museum if the entrance requirement for the museum is perfection?

Read *Steps to Christ*, page 62, about the condition for eternal life. Whose perfection is salvation based upon? Who's the broken pot?

How to Love Someone More

Does grace make you more or less eager to do good things?

Many people are afraid that when we accept grace we'll quit worrying about what's right and wrong for us to do. (See Romans 6:14-18.)

Read the story of Jesus at Simon's feast found in Luke 7:36-50. What do you think Jesus meant when He said, "He who has been forgiven little loves little" (verse 47)?

State the verse in the positive instead of the negative ("He who has been forgiven much . . . "). Can we accept Jesus' principle that concentrating on how much He has done for us makes us love *more*, not less?

What does this principle mean in your every day life? If you're having problems loving someone, or doing loving things for someone, should you try harder to love *them*, or think about how much Jesus loves *you*?

What other applications of the principle can you think of? How can it be meaningful to you today? How does this principle help you answer the first question in this section?

What is Grace Most Like for You?

Rank the following statements by putting a 1 in front of the statement you most agree with, and numbers 2-5 in front of the other statements, with 5 being the statement you like the least. Then share your rankings and discuss them.

Which is grace most like?

_____ God's acceptance of the past, allowing us to move into the future without guilt.

_____ God loving us with no strings attached.

_____ A reward from God.

_____ A gift from a best friend.

_____ God sharing love without requirements.[2]

The Light that Shines
from Every Truth

Here's an interesting thought from Ellen White:

"Every truth in the Word of God, from Genesis to Revelation, must be studied in the light that streams from the cross of Calvary." *Gospel Workers*, p. 315.

The grace of Christ is not *one* of our church's doctrines, but *the* truth upon which all other doctrines are based. Is that the way you understand our doctrines? Explore church doctrine (the second coming of Jesus, the seventh-day Sabbath, the inspiration of the Bible, for example) and discover how each subject is founded in grace. You may want to get some help from books such as *Seventh-day Adventists Believe*, *Anchor Points*, *Discover Jesus* or *A Reason to Believe*, all available from your Adventist Book Center.[3]

Grace Made Clear
by Contrast

The Bible often makes things plain to us through the use of a literary pattern known as contrasting parallelism, in which the second line of a verse says exactly the opposite of the first line. One of the best examples is found in Romans 6:23:

Line 1 - For the wages of sin is death;

Line 2 - But the gift of God is eternal life.

Write a contrasting parallel line for each of the following statements, then share your verses with your family:

• Line 1 - I sometimes think I can earn my way to heaven;

• Line 1 - Earthly friends often hold grudges;

• Line 1 - When I trust in myself, I end up worrying;

Now write a few parallelisms of your own. Write a new one every week or so. In a few months, collect the statements from all your family members and produce a family book with a desktop publishing program.

Jill, the Lion, and the Stream

Read the following story portion from C. S. Lewis' book for children called *The Silver Chair*[4]. The conversation happens when Jill meets Aslan, who represents Jesus.

"Are you not thirsty?" said the Lion.

"I'm *dying* of thirst," said Jill.

"Then drink," said the Lion.

"May I–could I–would you mind going away while I do?" said Jill.

The Lion answered this only by a look and a very low growl. And as Jill gazed at its motionless bulk, she realized that she might as well have asked the whole mountain to move aside for her convenience.

The delicious rippling noise of the stream was driving her nearly frantic.

"Will you promise not to–do anything to me, if I do come?" said Jill.

"I make no promise," said the Lion.

Jill was so thirsty now that, without noticing it, she had come a step nearer...

"I daren't come and drink," said Jill.

"Then you will die of thirst," said the Lion.

"Oh dear!" said Jill, coming another step nearer. "I suppose I must go and look for another stream then."

"There is no other stream," said the Lion.

Do you think that Aslan, the Lion, might have been referring to grace? Read Revelation 22:17 and see if you think the verse is talking about the same thing.

Create other metaphors or comparisons that, like the stream, describe the fullness of God's grace.

My Favorite Bible Picture of Grace

Choose a Bible story that illustrates grace to you and create a piece of art about the story. You could do a drawing, coloring, painting or sculpture.

Two good stories of grace to choose from are the Prodigal Son in Luke 15, and Jesus' reaction to the woman in John 8. See if one of these stories sparks your creativity.

God's Love Endures Forever

Use the responsive Scripture reading below in your family worship time. Assign one or more parts to each family member, depending on the number in your family. Practice reading with expression. Read the last line in triumphant unison.

The reading is adapted from [1]Isaiah 42:10-12; [2]24:14; [3]59:19; [4]Zechariah 2:10, 11; and [5]Psalm 107:1-3 (NIV).

Reader 1:
Sing to the Lord a new song,
His praise from the ends of the earth,

Reader 2:
Let the desert and its towns raise their voices.
Let them shout from the mountaintops.

Reader 3:
Let them give glory to the Lord
And proclaim His praise in the islands.[1]

Reader 4:
They raise their voices, they shout for joy;
From the west they acclaim the Lord's majesty.[2]

Reader 1:
And from the rising of the sun, they will revere His glory.[3]

Reader 2:
Shout and be glad, O daughter of Zion.
For I am coming, and I will live among you, declares the Lord.

Reader 3:
Many nations will be joined with the Lord in that day and will become My people.[4]

Reader 4:
Let the redeemed of the Lord say this–
those He redeemed from the hand of the foe,

Reader 1:
From east and west,

Reader 2:
From north and south.

Reader 3:
Give thanks to the Lord,

Reader 4:
For He is good;

All:
His love endures forever.[5]

Searching for Grace in the New Testament

The word "grace" is used 104 times in the New International Version of the New Testament. In each of the chapter combinations below, the word can be found six times.

Assign one of the passages to each member of your family who is old enough to take part. Agree to study your chapters for a week and then give a report to the family. During the week, do the following:

a. Locate each time the word "grace" is used.

b. Read and reread the passages until you really understand the meaning.

c. Ask your pastor to help you understand any passage that is unclear to you.

d. Prepare a report that explains how "grace" is used in your chapters, and what you learned from your study.

e. Finally, include a section in your report that reveals how your study can help make grace a more important part of your family life.

- Romans 3 and 5
- 2 Corinthians 8 and 9
- Galatians 1, 2 and 3
- Ephesians 1 and 2
- 1 Peter 1 and 5

Making Choices About Grace

An interesting way of identifying your feelings about grace is to be forced to choose between two options, both of which may be attractive to you. Look at the choices in the next column. Choose one option in each grouping. Then describe why you made the choice.

Grace is more like:
- an entree/a dessert
- a concert/a party
- snowfall/a tornado
- sunshine/moonlight
- a passport/a roadmap
- an application form/a final exam

Building Grace, One Word at a Time

An acrostic is a way of arranging words so that certain letters (usually the first letter of the word or line) form another word.

A single word acrostic formed on the word "grace" might look like this:

G - God's
R - Revelation
A - About
C - Choosing
E - Eternity

You can also build an acrostic one phrase or one sentence at a time, like this:

G - Great was our sin
R - Righteous was our God
A - Aware of our need
C - Christ came to save
E - Everyone who believes

Supply a piece of paper and a pen or pencil for everyone in your family. Construct an acrostic of your own, building on the word "grace." Choose either the one word form, or the phrase or sentence form.

[1] C. S. Lewis, *The Weight of Glory and Other Addresses* (New York, NY: McMillian, 1980), 92.

[2] Roland and Doris Larson, *Teaching Values* (Riverside, CA: La Sierra University Press, 1992).

[3] *Seventh-day Adventists Believe* (Washington, D.C.: Ministerial Association of the General Conference of Seventh-day Adventists, 1988); *Anchor Points* (Hagerstown, MD: Review and Herald Publishing Association, 1993); Chris Blake, editor, *A Reason to Believe* (Hagerstown, MD: Review and Herald Publishing Association, 1993); Mark Finley, *Discover Jesus* (Fallbrook, CA: Hart Research Center, 1993).

[4] C. S. Lewis, *The Silver Chair* (New York, NY: Collier Books, 1953), pages 16, 17.

Additional Activities to Help
Establish a Grace Orientation

On these pages, record activities which your family creates to help establish a grace orientation in your home.

_____

_____

_____

_____

_____

_____

_____

_____

_____

_____

_____

_____

_____

_____

_____

_____

_____

_____

_____

_____

_____

_____

_____

_____

_____

_____

_____

_____

_____

_____

Discovering the Joy of Worship

Finding Solutions in a Brainstorm

Brainstorming is an active method of discovering many solutions to a common problem. The rules are simple:

a. Pose a dilemma that needs to be solved.

b. Invite everyone to contribute ideas for the solution. No idea is unworthy. No idea gets criticized. The more ideas the better.

c. Keep track of all the ideas you can generate in 5 minutes. When the time is up, prioritize your list. Which ideas do you like best?

Why not brainstorm with your family about times of family worship? Here are some questions to brainstorm together:

• What would make family worship most meaningful for you?

• What topics would you like to study and discuss?

• What activities would interest you the most?

• What would be the best time of day to have worship?

What Can We Learn from Television?

Record your favorite family TV show. Choose a program every member of the family agrees is a good program.

Then play the program again the next night. But this time, watch for values statements. Pause the program frequently and ask questions such as: "What did she mean when she said that?" "Is that the way we want to relate to the topic?" "How can we adopt the same values?" or, "How can we be sure we don't accept the same standard?"

Travelling to the Holy Land

Go to a travel agent or a video store and obtain a video on the land of Israel. Watch the video together. What parts of today's country do you recognize from Bible stories? Did you see the Lake of Galilee? Jerusalem? Bethlehem? Jericho? Joppa? What other places sound familiar to you?

Where would you like to travel in the Holy Land? To the town of Nazareth? Or Capernaum? Would you like to see where Samuel grew up? Or where Gideon lived? Or Mary and Martha's home in Bethany? How about a trip through Hezekiah's tunnel?

Imagine a family vacation in Israel. Get maps and travel brochures and check out books from your library. How would you organize a two week stay? Plan the routes you'd travel and the places you'd stay.

When your itinerary is complete, pretend that you've actually left on the trip. Each day talk about what you'd be doing if you really were in Israel. Look at pictures of just the area you would have visited. Find Bible stories about these places.

You may also want to plan such a trip to Egypt, Greece and Rome and follow in the footsteps of Jesus, Joseph, Peter and Paul.

Keeping a Journal of Worship Experiences

Begin keeping a daily journal of your worship experiences. Write in the journal a summary of those times during the week when you feel you really enter into worship. You may want to keep track of the following types of experiences:

a. Times when you are overwhelmed with gratitude for God's blessings to you and your family.

b. Times when you are convinced you are in God's presence.

c. Times when you are sure of God's leading in your decisions.

d. Times when your service to others is selfless and worshipful.

e. Times when others, including other family members, convey God's love to you in words, deeds or just by being there.

f. Times when you open your heart to God in complaint, discouragement or agony and find comfort.

Occasionally, share entries from your journal with your family. Your thoughts will encourage them to keep their own journal and to share their worship moments.

When I Get to Heaven

Play the "When I Get to Heaven" game together. Turn the lights down low, play some sacred music quietly in the background, get comfortable and imagine what it will be like to be in the earth made new.

In addition to Jesus, what Bible characters do you want to get to know? Who would you like to visit with from the pages of world history? Are there friends or relatives who have died that you can't wait to see again? What activities will you plan for yourself? How far would you like to travel? Don't be shy about creating the most fantastic images you can imagine.

When you're through, thank Jesus for making it possible for these heavenly dreams to come true.

Worship Experiences in the Bible

The Bible is full of wonderful examples of worship experiences. Assign one of the passages in the next column to each family member. Spend an evening exploring the verses. What does the passage teach us about worship? How can we incorporate the lessons of the biblical experiences of worship into our own worship experiences?

Bring a report on your passage to another session of family worship.

- The Worship of the Wise Men; Matthew 2:1-11.
- Paul's Instruction in the Marketplace of Athens; Acts 17:16-31.
- Worship in Heaven's Throne Room; Revelation 4:1-11.
- The Psalmist's Reasons for Worship; Psalm 95:1-7.
- A New Song About Worship; Psalm 96:1-13.
- Giving Thanks in Worship; Psalm 100:1-5.

Studying the Bible, One Book at a Time

There are, of course, many ways to study the Bible. One of the most fascinating is to take an entire book of the Bible and read through it from beginning to end. This is especially interesting to do in the great story books of the Bible, such as Genesis, Judges, Ruth and Acts.

You may enjoy setting aside one night of the week just to read a Bible book. Read for an agreed upon amount of time, or until you come to a natural stopping place. Then don't read again from that book until the same night next week.

Another Bible book that's easy to read is the book of Proverbs. Since the book has 31 chapters, you can always read the chapter that corresponds to the current day of the month. Be sure to talk about the meanings of the proverbs as you read them. And discuss how you can apply the proverbs in your home.

Creating Joy with Simple Bible Games

Sometimes the simplest games give families the greatest pleasure. Here are a few simple Bible games you can play during family worship to create a joyful, meaningful experience that is also informative and inspirational.

• Play a game of 20 Questions. Help your kids ask questions that will increase their understanding of biblical time-lines: Old or New Testament? In the book of Genesis? In the period of the Kings? And so on.

• Create a Bible Character Chain in which the first letter of the new character matches the last letter of the last character. A chain might look like this: Abel, **Lot, Tho**mas, **S**amuel, etc. Sit in a circle and have each person choose a character when it's his or her turn.

• Make a crossword puzzle with words that appear in the Bible. Put the words into the puzzle first, then create the clues, including Bible verses to look up.

Singing the Hymns Ahead of Time

Sometime in the middle of the week, call your church secretary and ask him or her to tell you the hymns that have been chosen for this week's worship service. Then spend an evening singing the hymns together before Sabbath. Try to memorize at least the first and last verses of the hymns so you can sing them with all your hearts when you get to them in the church service.

You'll also find it interesting to look up stories about how the hymns came to be written and composed. There is a companion volume to the *SDA Hymnal* which tells the stories[1]. Or you can find similar books about popular hymns at a Christian book store. When you know the stories, you'll find the hymns will be more meaningful to every member of your family.

Worshipping God in Everything We Do

One of the tragedies of today's busy life is that we seem to have relegated worship to *times* of worship. We go to Sabbath School and church to worship. We have family worship. But then we get on with the rest of our life. We have successfully segmented our worship from all the other things we do.

But, the biblical worship ideal is that we worship God with all our heart and soul and strength (Deut. 6:5), with everything we do (Romans 12:1 and Colossians 3:17).

Discuss how we can worship God in the other aspects of our life.

- Employment
- Family relationships
- The things we eat and drink
- Schoolwork
- Entertainment
- Recreation

Seeing God Through Other People's Eyes

One the best ways to deepen your understanding of worship is to talk to people from different cultures and ethnic backgrounds from yours. Visit an ethnic worship service, even if the service is conducted in a different language. Observe how the people respond to the music, how they pray, how they take part in the service. If there is a visitor's potluck after the service, stay and sample new varieties of food.

Another way to accomplish this same goal is to interview people in your community, perhaps even in your own church, who grew up in a different country. Ask them about their earliest worship memories. Ask them what they were taught about how to worship and when to worship. Invite them to sing a song or pray for you in their native language. Talk to them about how they view God.

Draw some conclusions on how broad and inclusive worship can be.

A Christian's View on Contemporary Issues

Discuss an important contemporary issue. Choose from topics such as abortion, conservation, human or civil rights, the death penalty, gun control, and freedom of speech.

Where should Christians get their information on these topics? What should be the basis for Christian opinions on contemporary issues? Should Christians be active in political and social movements?

How should the church respond? Should it tell us what to believe on each issue, or give us guidelines, or just hope we make good decisions? How does our Christianity impact our opinions on these issues?

You may want to explore the issues in magazines such as *Insight* and *Group* before you have your discussion. Keep the conversation positive and friendly.

Favorite Bible Verses of My Grandparents

Make a phone call to your grandparents to find out what are their favorite Bible passages. Take notes on their answers when you ask them the following questions:

a. Who is your favorite Bible character? What part of his or her life do you most enjoy reading about?

b. What is your favorite memory verse? When did you first memorize it? How has the verse helped you from time to time?

c. Do you remember a time from your childhood when you were asked to read the Bible in public or recite a verse? Were you nervous? Did you do a good job?

d. If you were going to commit an entire book of the Bible to memory, what book would it be?

Share your notes with the family. Look up your grandparents favorite verses and characters and read them together. Write a thank-you note to your grandparents.

Studying the Sabbath School Lesson Together

This week in Sabbath School make sure each family member gets a copy of the resource which contains their Sabbath School lesson. During the week, ask everyone to study their lesson and be prepared to share highlights of the lesson.

Then, on Friday night, when you have a little more time than usual, ask each family member questions about their lesson. Ask questions such as: "What was special to you about what you studied?" "What part did you not understand?" "How is the lesson important to us this week?"

Illustrating the Fruits of the Spirit

Buy a set of finger paints, inexpensive water colors, or even a new box of crayons. Select one of the fruits of the Spirit (you'll find the list in Galatians 5:22, 23) and paint or color a scene that represents the fruit you've chosen.

Lessons from a Walk Around the Block

Take a walk together outside. On the way, look for things that could illustrate the life and challenges of a growing Christian.

If there are preschoolers among you, allow them to choose the most obvious items, such as a flower or a blade of grass. Be creative. Collect all the items you choose, but don't pick up anything that obviously belongs to someone. Then return home and discuss your object lessons. See if you can find a Bible text about each item.

You Remind Me of God's Love

It's always a good idea to look for the best in others, especially the people we live with. There are behaviors we appreciate for contributing to a peaceful atmosphere in our homes. And there are actions that we like because they remind us of how much God loves us.

Sit together in a tight circle and finish this sentence, "Mom reminds me of God's love when she..." Have each family member complete the sentence. Then start a new round of appreciation for each one present.

When you pray tonight, thank God for your family.

Exploring Bible Doctrines

Many times we catch our theology from our pastors in church or from our teachers in school instead of developing our theology from our own Bible study. How can we become more active in our beliefs? How can we have God's truths written in our hearts?

Family worship is a wonderful place to start. Ask your family members what Bible topics they'd like to study. Or what doctrinal subjects they feel they need help in understanding. After you've made a list, prioritize the topics by voting on which subjects you'd like to study first. Then set aside one evening a week to explore each subject.

Here's a list of proposed topics: the grace of God, the inspiring way God communicates with us, the Godhead's plan to save us, the incarnation of Jesus, the second coming of Jesus, the gift of the Holy Spirit, and the never-ending joys of heaven.

One of the best resources for your study is *Insight* magazine's *A Reason to Believe*. This Bible study aid is full of activities to help you understand Bible doctrine. You'll find the book in your ABC.

First Things First: A Chronological Study

Take a Bible, a piece of paper, and a pen or pencil into separate areas of the house where no one else can observe your study. Choose a section of the Bible (like Genesis, the Gospels, Acts or 1 and 2 Kings) and look for ten significant events. If you choose Genesis, for example, you might choose these events: the creation, the death of Abel, the flood, the destruction of Sodom and Gomorrah, Abraham sacrificing Isaac, the marriage of Isaac and Rebekah, etc.

When you have your list of ten, scramble them up! Rewrite the list so no one will be able to tell the proper chronological order. Then call everyone back together and exchange lists.

Now try to put the lists back in order. Which event on the list took place first? Which one is next? Keep working until you have the entire list in correct chronological order. When you're ready ask the person who scrambled the list to check your order.

A More Meaningful Prayer Life

Here are a few ideas on how to make your family prayer life more meaningful.

Remember that prayer is not just asking God for favors or telling Him the things you want. Prayer begins in praise. What do you have to thank God for today? What are the blessings you realize He's given you? Ask everyone to express thanksgiving for one thing God has done.

Remember, too, that prayer is most powerful when it is specific. Try being more to the point and less general in your prayers.

Pray around a circle in short sentences. Don't feel compelled to be lengthy and eloquent. Express just one thought in your own words.

And pray for each other.

Great Art Illustrates How God Lives with Us

Go to a library and locate a good book on religious art. Try to find one with lots of pictures of paintings and sculptures throughout the centuries. Check out the book and set aside some time to look at the art work together.

What periods of art do you like the best? Is there a particular artist whose work you really appreciate? Can you find a favorite picture?

Notice how many artists paint Biblical characters in the clothing and settings of the artist's own time. That's the "incarnation principle," the word becoming flesh and dwelling among us (see John 1:14).

As we study the Bible, we'll also find that its message is most powerful when we apply it to our lives today, as we let it come to life in the settings of our lives.

The Witness of the Waldensians

Research the lives of the medieval Protestants known as Waldensians. They lived in France and northern Italy and faced fierce persecution because of their beliefs. The stories of their courage in face of danger, their commitment in spite of opposition, and their loyalty to each other continue to be among the most inspiring tales of Christian witness anywhere in the world.

As you find books to read about the Waldensians, also buy a map that shows northern Italy in detail. Locate the town of Torre Pellice, west of Torino (Turin). Today a Waldensian college operates in Torre Pellice. Just a few miles to the north is the tiny village of Pra del Torno, the last place of refuge in many times of persecution, and the location of the original Waldensian seminary. Also try to locate on your map the Po River. As you read the stories of the Waldensians, watch for mentions of the river.

The Inspiration of Musical Worship

What's your favorite Christian song? Is it an old hymn that you first learned when you were a child? Or a current song by a contemporary Christian musician? A classical piece by one of the giants of serious music? Or a campfire chorus that's connected to special memories?

Bring those memories and that favorite song to worship, along with the favorites of the other members of your family. Listen to the song on CD or tape. Play it again and sing along. Then reflect on the meaning of the words. Analyze the contribution the music makes to the message. Describe your feelings as you listen to the song. And discuss why music is such an inspirational part of the worship experience.

Remember not to be critical of other people's musical choices. Endeavor to find the best in the favorites you listen to in this activity.

A Paragraph from Your Favorite Writer

Our world is blessed by the talents of hundreds of inspirational writers. Surely you have found one individual whose writing never ceases to inspire you.

Find a paragraph which you consider particularly meaningful and share it with your family. Ask them also to share a passage from a writer they enjoy and admire.

Here's a paragraph from a collection of C. S. Lewis's sermons and addresses. The passage always makes me long to be in heaven:

> "At present we are on the outside of the world, the wrong side of the door. We discern the freshness and purity of morning, but they do not make us fresh and pure. We cannot mingle with the splendours we see. But all the leaves of the New Testament are rustling with the rumour that it will not always be so. Some day, God willing, we shall get *in*."[2]

Finding New Life in New Bibles

Bible study never ceases to delight and challenge our minds. But, sometimes we feel like we've heard it all before. Why not explore the Bible in a new version, a different one from the one you are most familiar with. Many people find the new phrasing of contemporary versions invigorating, revealing old, familiar thoughts in fresh, new ways.

One of the most delightful new paraphrases is called *The Message; the New Testament in Contemporary English*. Written by Eugene H. Peterson and published in 1993 by NavPress, *The Message* speaks to us in the words of our day. Take a look at the parable of the prodigal son to see the power and energy of this Bible.

Two editions of the New International Version are particularly helpful to families attempting to establish a regular worship pattern. One is *The Serendipity Bible* published by Serendipity House in 1986. This edition includes marginal questions to help you discuss the Bible passages you've been reading; questionnaires on 48 different Bible stories; ten study courses, each with six sessions in beginning and advanced levels; and a helpful subject index.

Another wonderful study aid is *The Family Worship Bible*. Published by Holman Bible Publishers in 1991, this edition includes articles on God's plan for families, how to find God's will for your family, and how to conduct family Bible study and worship. There are 52 age-graded weekly family worship suggestions, discussions on contemporary topics (from AIDS to teen issues to violence), activities, prayer ideas and even songs to sing.

Why not spend some time in your local Christian book store and bring home a new Bible for your family to enjoy.

---

[1] Wayne Hooper and Edward E. White, *Companion to the Seventh-day Adventist Hymnal* (Hagerstown, MD: Review and Herald Pubishing, 1988).

[2] C. S. Lewis, *The Weight of Glory, and Other Adresses* (New York, NY: McMillian, 1980).

Additional Activities to Help Discover the Joy of Worship

On these pages, record activities which your family creates to help discover the joy of worship in your home.

_____

_____

_____

_____

_____

_____

_____

_____

_____

_____

_____

_____

_____

_____

_____

_____

_____

_____

_____

_____

_____

_____

_____

_____

_____

_____

_____

_____

_____

_____

_____

_____

_____

_____

_____

_____

The Colors of Grace in Our Homes

Creating a Faith Community

How Families Support Spiritual Growth

When we talk about a faith community, we're referring to a place where individuals find encouragement and support as they grow as Christians. This happens in schools, in churches, and most assuredly, in our families, where the climate for faith development is crucial.

To demonstrate the importance of this climate, choose a doorway in your home with a surface you can work on to record family height. Measure each family member and make a mark on the doorway surface. Then discuss how each person in the family is a different height, and how each person will grow at a different rate. What will the family do to make sure the family continues growing? Describe the nutrients you'll need. And the changes in clothing as you grow.

What are the equivalent factors in spiritual growth? What are the nutrients we need? How can the family support spiritual growth?

The Bible's View of Community

Before we go any further, let's explore what the Bible has to say about the subject of community.

In the column to the right are six Bible passages which contain principles of successfully creating a faith community. Assign one of the passages to each member of your family. Spend an evening examining the verses. Then discuss the passages together.

What are the principles you've discovered? Does the passage invite action or contemplation? What can you do in your home to put the principles to work?

- John 13:34, 35
- Romans 14:13
- Romans 15:1-7
- Galatians 6:9, 10
- Philippians 2:1-4
- 1 John 1:7

Community Goals for God's People

Read the following Bible passages and list the community goals God has for His people. How many of the goals have to do with your personal spiritual advancement? How many deal with your relationship with others? What are the stated purposes of the goals?

Select several of the goals and discuss specific actions that will help you reach those goals. For example, how can your family respond to this verse: "…be patient, bearing with one another in love." (Ephesians 4:2) What do those words mean for you? Can you think of family circumstances which demand patience? In what ways could you "bear with one another" more successfully?

Imagine what the atmosphere would be like if your family attained these goals.

- Ephesians 4:2-7
- Ephesians 4:11-16
- Ephesians 4:25-32
- Colossians 3:11-17

A Family Reunion Worship

If your family lives close to grandparents, invite them to your house for a special family reunion worship. Ask the grandparents to be prepared to answer questions about their younger days.

Without other distractions to keep you from listening, invite your grandparents to reminisce about these types of experiences: Tell us about the town where you grew up. What type of work did your parents do? Where were they born? What's your happiest childhood memory?

What do you remember about your elementary school? Did you play in a band or sing in a choir? Did you take part in school sports? Do you recall your graduation?

Tell us about how the two of you met. What did you do on your first date? Where did you work while you were going to high school? What was your first job after school?

What do you remember about the church you attended? When were you baptized? What was the best part about having Christian friends? What was most challenging about being a Christian?

To conlude, thank God for your grandparents and for the Christian example they've provided for you. Ask them to pray, too.

Adopting a New Set of "Grandparents"

If your own grandparents don't live nearby, or if your relatives aren't Christian and would be uncomfortable answering the questions above, why not adopt new grandparents. Think of the people in your church who are older and don't have nearby family to visit. Invite them to your house and get better acquainted. After a couple of visits, tell them about wanting to have a family reunion worship and go through the questions above. You'll make wonderful new friends.

Exploring Your Family Through Art

Let's get all the family artists to work to explore our community.

Complete a little research on your family tree, ascertaining countries of origin, ancestral careers and common genealogical patterns (every one was tall, dark and handsome, for example). Then design a piece of art that illustrates your family heritage.

You may design a family crest with the traditional four sections to a shield. Or create a banner with symbols and words that represent your family. You could stitch a wall-hanging, paint a poster, or even come up with a catchy bumper sticker.

Don't forget to include your spiritual roots.

Getting Acquainted with Family Job Sites

The distances between us that sometimes seem so great are often a result of ignorance rather than intention. Research shows that children have almost no idea of their parents' occupations. And parents are seldom seen inside their kids' classrooms, unless it's to pick up grades, or to be told about a discipline problem. We sometimes don't even know the names of each other's friends.

Let's put an end to such ignorance! Arrange for a few hours during the work week (this will probably work best in the summertime when school's out) when the kids (perhaps one at a time would be best) visit their parents' job sites and get a firsthand, close-up look at the work Mom and Dad do.

Then arrange a visit to school during classes and sit quietly in the back of the classroom. Or, if that's too embarrassing to the kids, spend the evening helping with homework, reviewing for tests, etc. Both experiences will be eye openers.

Accepting People Who are Different

Roleplay a situation where a couple of teenagers with extreme tastes in clothing and hairstyle walk into church to be met by an older couple who have the assignment to be this week's greeters.

Who's going to volunteer to take the part of the teenagers? Maybe the parents would like this assignment. The kids would have a great time dressing the "teens" and moussing their hair into the wildest styles possible.

And who will be the older couple? Maybe these roles should be played by the youngest in the family. Dress up in a conservative suit and dress and apply a little talcum powder to turn the hair gray.

Now roleplay two situations. In one, have the greeters express their disapproval of the teens. What would the older folks say or do to show they don't like the way the kids have dressed for church? Have the greeters be completely non-accepting.

Next, roleplay the opposite situation in which the greeters don't even notice the way the kids are dressed and welcome them warmly to church. How do the greeters act? What do they say? How does their acceptance change the feelings of the teens?

After the roleplay, discuss what you learned about acceptance of people who are different from you.

Write Specific Notes of Encouragement

Practice the fine art of writing notes of encouragement. Keep the notes simple; just a couple of sentences will be enough to express your gratitude. Make them to the point. Be specific about what makes you happy. And don't connect the encouragement with any past behavior you didn't like. Write a note to each family member each week.

Strengthening Family Traditions

Family traditions celebrate a heritage of togetherness and joy, and often last for generations as the tradition is repeated over and over again by family members.

Many times the tradition is centered in holidays, and frequently it has to do with food. In my home, my wife, whose father is of Swedish ancestry, prepares a sweet, Swedish rice pudding for breakfast on Christmas day. Christmas just wouldn't seem like Christmas to us if it didn't begin with that delicious treat.

What are the traditions in your home? Become more aware of your own regular practices. Or begin now to establish new traditions.

And here's a suggestion to add to your holiday list: keep track of the baptismal dates of every family member. On the Sabbath closest to that date, begin a tradition of doing something special. Serve a favorite meal. Look at pictures of the baptism. Recall the events and feelings of the day. And give a gift that will contribute to the continuing spiritual growth of the honoree.

Conversations About Spiritual Challenges

One of the clearest findings in the *Valuegenesis* research had to do with how our youth perceive their parents' spirituality. Our children believe we are comfortable talking about our religion, and they indicate we converse about our religion frequently. Unfortunately, however, we get low marks when it comes to listening to them about the challenges of *their* religious experience.

Obviously we need to do a better job at conveying our genuine interest in their spiritual growth. Start listening to your conversations with other family members. Are they too one-sided? Stop what you're doing, make eye contact, and *listen*.

Five Family Comparisons

Choose one of each pair of words or phrases in the next column which you feel best represents the true meaning of family. All answers are correct; listen to the reasons behind the choices.

Family is most like:
• a locked gate/an open door.
• a color/a sound.
• a reward/an invitation.
• virtual reality/remote control.
• a school/a church.

Let's Go on a Picnic

Put together a family picnic basket. Shop for a basket and for a dinnerware set with different colored plates and glasses, one color for each member of the family. At the grocery store send each family member after a different item: napkins, sandwich filling, fruit, drinks, dessert, etc. Make the lunch together. Don't forget a table cloth and bug repellant. Plan an afternoon off together and really enjoy yourselves.

I'd Like to Hear a Sermon About. . .

Make a list of subjects you'd like to hear your pastor preach a sermon about. Write a short paragraph about your interest in each topic. Your list may include Bible passages you don't fully understand, contemporary issues, suggestions for deepening your devotional life, or any other spiritual topic that's on your mind.

When your list reaches ten topics, give it to your pastor, along with a note of appreciation for all his or her hard work.

If You Were in Charge of the Church

Imagine that you were suddenly given charge of the denomination. You could have any position you wanted. You could redesign the structure or leave it just like it is. You could combine any job descriptions, or eliminate jobs or create new ones. You could hire people you know, allocate budget for projects you feel are important, send money to institutions or mission fields, or declare new directions for the church.

If such an opportunity were yours, what would you do? What would be your first action? To whom would you turn for advice? How would you communicate your decisions to church members in the local churches?

How would you involve the youth of the church? What challenges could you help them with? What issues would you hope they could solve?

Demonstrating Love for Challenged Christians

There are times in our lives when our need for Christian community is at its greatest. Generally those times are times of crisis or times of loss: separation or divorce, financial hardship, the death of a family member, the oppression of addictive or abusive behavior, or trouble with the authorities.

Unfortunately, there are still church members who feel the church is a rest home for saints who have stopped having problems, instead of a hospital for combatants in the great controversy between good and evil. When we ignore, or fail to include people whose Christian experience is being challenged, we do not act in love as Christ would have us act (1 John 3:11-18).

What can your family do to demonstrate love to the challenged Christians in your church or community?

The Gift of a Great, New Book

Save the money to buy your pastor or the principal of your school a new book. Do some snooping to discover the type of book he or she enjoys reading and what books are already in this person's library.

Then wrap the book in the cheeriest wrapping paper you can find and slip the present onto the person's desk at church or at school. Have everyone in your family sign a card to attach to the package.

A Connection with the Mission Field

Make a connection between someone in your church and the mission field: a son or daughter who's serving as a student missionary, people who used to be members who are now missionaries, a former student in your school who's now on mission assignment.

Take pictures of the people in church, have each member of your family write a note, and send the package to the missionary, explaining that you still think of them often. But don't stop there. Repeat the package at holidays and after special church functions.

Remembering Church Members in the Military

You may have church members who are serving in the military. Such members are often forgotten by your church family. So take it upon yourself to keep the ties strong. Set a time each month to write. And make the holidays special by sending cards and gifts. Also find out the birthdate of the member and send a birthday card and gift.

Harmony, Unison and Unity

Demonstrate the differences between the words "unison" and "harmony." Sing the song "Jesus Loves Me" together two times through. The first time, sing in unison, everyone singing the melody on the same note. The second time, sing in harmony, adding alto, tenor and bass notes to the soprano melody.

Which time through did you enjoy the most? What are the benefits of singing in unison? What are the drawbacks? How is harmony different? Which way is easier? Which way is more difficult?

Is unison necessary for unity? Read Colossians 3:13-15. What proceeds unity? What follows?

What are the spiritual implications of this demonstration?

Online Searches for Community

If your computer is connected to an online information service (such as "Internet," *Compuserve*™, or *America Online*™) you already know of the incredible access you have to information. If you haven't yet subscribed to one of these services, this would be a great time to get better acquainted with such a program.

Search the recent listings of news magazines. *Time*, for example, and *U.S. News and World Report*, are both available online. Look for articles which tell the stories of communities which came together in the face of violence, educational challenge, community service projects, or natural disasters (the tornado that struck the church in Goshen, Alabama, the floods of the midwest, or southern California's earthquakes).

Read the stories you find. What are the common denominators of community action? What are the benefits of working together instead of working by yourself? How can we apply these lessons to our spiritual experience?

Community Action
in *Chariots of Fire*

One of the most beloved films of all times is the 1981 British movie, *Chariots of Fire*. This remarkable true story follows the lives of Eric Liddell, a Scottish son of missionaries to China, and Harold Abrahams, a Jew whose father is an immigrant to England from Lithuania. Both young men represent their country in the 1924 Paris Olympics.

In one of the most riveting scenes in the film, Liddell refuses to run his Olympic race on the Sabbath. In spite of intense pressure from the members of the British Olympic Committee, including the Prince of Wales, Liddell's faith endures.

If you haven't seen the film in a while, rent it and view it together. After the scene in which Liddell is pressured to run, stop the movie and talk about what you've just watched. What is the source of the community which solves the dilemma? How does such community supersede nationality or language? Why did one type of community action fail to change Liddell's mind while another type of community action won the day?

What implications does the story have for young people today who are pressured to abandon their belief system?

Creative Expressions
of Community

Set aside an evening to creatively write about your gratitude for genuine community.

Compose a few pieces of Haiku poetry that tell of the security and acceptance of a faith community. Talk about how the faith development process is encouraged. Write a rhyme or an acrostic which expresses your delight with the community provided by the members of your family. Or write a descriptive paragraph about a time when you realized the joys of community.

Critical Thinking Skills

A community functions not only to make its members feel accepted, but also to challenge their thinking. In an active faith community, people feel free to explore their faith, to ask tough questions, and to evaluate traditions. Questioners don't fear reprisal or exclusion because they are seeking truth. In fact, a caring faith community understands that making our faith our own is a necessary step in the faith maturity process.

As your family discusses Christianity's response to the challenging issues of our day, encourage each member to ask specific questions that help clarify the issue and lead to truth-filled conclusions.

Here is a summary of critical thinking skills to help in this process. Apply these skills frequently.

1. **Defining the Issue**
   * Identify central points
   * Compare distinctive attributes
   * Determine relevant information
   * Ask clarifying questions
2. **Understanding the Issue**
   * Distinguish fact from opinion
   * Check context and consistency
   * Identify unstated assumptions
   * Recognize cliches and stereotypes
   * Recognize bias and propaganda
   * Recognize value orientations
3. **Drawing Conclusions**
   * Determine data adequacy
   * Predict probable consequences

Community is Based on the Work of Jesus

React to the following statement by Dietrich Bonhoeffer. It's found on page 26 of his book *Life Together; A Discussion of Christian Fellowship* (published in 1954 by Harper and Row). What meaning does the statement hold for your family?

"The more genuine and the deeper our community becomes, the more will everything else between us recede, the more clearly and purely will Jesus Christ and his work become the one and only thing that is vital between us."

Additional Activities to Help Create a Faith Community

On these pages, record activities which your family creates to help build a faith community in your home.

Encouraging a Life of Service

The Bible Teaches Us to Serve

Ask each member of your family to explore one of the following Bible passages and identify fundamental principles about service. What do the verses tell us about how God feels about our serving others? What can be the long-lasting results of our service? How do these verses help motivate you to serve?

Discuss the principles in your family and determine how you can apply the principles in your own service.

- Our Service is to Jesus;
  Matthew 25:31-40
- Jesus Describes His Mission;
  Luke 4:18-21.
- Service Opportunities in the
  Early Church;
  Acts 2:41-47.
- Gifts for Service;
  Ephesians 4:11-15.
- Generosity Results in Thanks-
  giving;
  2 Corinthians 9:11-13.

A Family Service Inventory

Conduct a family service inventory. See how much of the necessary service ingredients you have at your house:

• A willingness to put your faith into action.

• The time to make someone else happy.

• A vision of your family working together.

• A desire to be part of an active, winning Christianity.

• A good imagination to create your own service opportunities.

Now talk about the work around the house that each of you are responsible for. Listen for jobs you'd be willing to do occasionally, including the jobs we take for granted, such as filling the car with gas, taking out the trash, making supper, and cleaning the bath tub.

The Heroes of Christian Service

Compile a list of the heroes of Christian service. Individuals on your list may be family members or friends, people from your church or a church you used to attend, or people from the community in which you live. Your heroes can be current or historical.

As you add to your list, search the library and Christian book store for books about these people. Begin to build a family library of service. Here are a couple of recommenda-

tions for your collection:

• Frank and Janet Ferrell, *Trevor's Place* (San Francisco, CA: Harper & Row, 1985).

• Steve Case & Fred Cornforth, *We Are His Hands* (Carmichael, CA: 1994).

Also pick up copies of *The Random Acts of Kindness* series (by the editors of Conari Press, 1993), delightful little books full of stories of service and quotations about kindness and compassion.

Service Projects in Your Community

Interview community service organizations to discover the types of service projects taking place in your town. Be sure to ask which programs are open to volunteers.

Don't forget that your own church probably has an active community service program. Also, talk to the community liaison officer of the public school districts in your community. These organizations often have well-developed programs for which you may be able to volunteer (such as tutoring).

Add these opportunities to your growing service projects list.

Getting Ready to Serve

Decide together what the best way is for your family to become involved in service projects. Should you devote one evening a week? Or will the weekends be the best time for you? Do you want to plan the things you do for others, but surprise each other with projects at home? Or should those home projects also be planned?

As you look through the ideas in this section of this book, additional ideas will come to mind. Write down those project ideas so you won't forget them. And add projects you hear other people taking part in.

Make a shopping list of supplies you'll need to complete the projects you've decided upon. Is this the week you're going to make sandwiches for the homeless? You'll need to buy extra bread and fixings. Are you going to paint a fence? Get the paint ahead of time.

You'll find that the anticipation of the project, including buying supplies, will inspire every one of your family members.

Sprucing Up the Family Car

Set aside 45 minutes or so to do a surprise first-class job of cleaning one of your family cars. In addition to washing the car, vacuum, wash the windows, empty the trash from under the seats, and clean out the trunk. Apply a little wax and scrub the tires. Then present the keys to the driver with an extra flourish: a flower, candy bar or thank you note for all the safe miles driven.

A Surprise Project in Your Own Front Yard

Take a long, critical look at your yard, analyzing the possibilities for colorful landscaping, clean-up needs, and new design. Get up early on Sunday morning and accomplish one of these tasks before everyone else wakes up. Then, let the family discover the changes on their own.

A Sparkling Night Off from the Dishwashing

Who usually does the supper dishes in your home? Why not give this person a much needed break from the normal routine.

As you finish your evening meal together, announce that this is a night off from the usual pattern of dishwashing. Escort the person who normally does the dishes to a comfortable chair and hand him or her the newspaper or a new magazine or the remote control to the TV. Make a big deal about this being a night off.

Then, take the time to do the best dishwashing ever. Take care of all the little details until the kitchen is spotless and sparkling.

A Special Family
Service Coupon

Design a family service coupon for someone in your family. Draw a decorative border and apply some color. Write a message that shows appreciation and invites the person's choice in your project ("Good for one hour's project of your choice," for example). Put your coupon in an envelope and place it under the pillow of the person you're giving the project to. Or address the envelope, put a stamp on it and mail it.

Starting the Morning
in Style

Prepare breakfast in bed this weekend for someone in your family. Don't connect it to a holiday or a birthday. Just do it for fun. Plan ahead and buy the person's favorite breakfast food. Present it with a linen napkin and a flower in a vase.

Even cold cereal and toast taste better when presented with love and style.

A Friendly Batch of
Fresh Cookies

Bake a batch of cookies together to give to someone in your church who doesn't have family members living nearby. Choose your favorite recipe. Involve everyone in the family in buying the ingredients, preparing the batter, and baking the cookies. Then put the cookies in an unusual package: a colorful ceramic or tin container, a decorative box, or a cellophane bag.

While the cookies are still warm deliver them, along with a carton of cold milk or a container of hot chocolate. Take the time to enjoy your gift with its recipient.

Preparing the Food
for a Feeding Program

Locate a feeding program in your community that needs some extra food, as well as the people to serve the food. Your church may have such a program. Or there may be a shelter in town that needs some help. Find out from the managers of the program what the menu calls for, then purchase the food and prepare it together. The best part will be watching the smiles as you serve the food.

Around the Block
Work-Bee

Organize a work bee for your neighborhood. Plan the work that needs to be done. Include pulling weeds from unsightly flower beds, sweeping next to the curbs, picking up trash, and maybe even planting some fresh flowers.

Invite all your neighbors to take part. Work together for an hour or two. Prepare a couple of pitchers of cold lemonade to refresh everyone.

After the project, take time to write a thank you note to everyone who took part.

Corresponding with
a Student Missionary

Obtain a list of student missionaries from the Adventist college nearest you or from your conference youth director. Choose a student you know or one that is serving in a country you're interested in.

Every month or so, spend a Sabbath afternoon writing a letter to your selected missionary. Ask questions about the type of work he or she is doing. And share stories about your family service projects.

Reading to Nursing Home Residents

Find a nursing home nearby your house that will allow you to come in some afternoon or evening and read to the residents. Interview a couple of people who would be interested in listening to you read. Determine what the best schedule would be for them. Then choose a story and keep your appointment.

Open a Community Bicycle Shop

Set up a community bicycle repair shop to service the bikes of the kids in your neighborhood. Open for a couple of hours each weekend and invite the kids to come in to repair or pump up their tires, tighten their brakes, or just to add a little oil.

Ask other community people to join you in keeping the bicycles operating well. The neighborhood kids will help with the marketing of your service. You may want to create some safety quizzes to help the bikers keep focused on riding safely.

Adopt a Room or Part of a Park

Adopt a room in your church or school, or a corner of a public park. Take the responsibility to keep the room or the park clean and in good condition. From time to time you may need to paint the room or plant some flowers in the park. Be sure to check with the proper authorities to see if there are any restrictions.

Take pictures before and after each project you undertake. Post the photographs in or near the room. Or video tape the project, including lots of close-up shots of the participants.

Before and After School Service

Check with the administration office of your school to see if there are any children who have to walk long distances to or from school, or who have to stay home alone for extended time periods after school.

Offer to provide transportation for these students. Invite them to spend an afternoon a week with you. Or spend one day a week at their house. Be sure to clear your plans with the parents and with your school.

Visiting Kids in the Hospital

Every day of the week there are children confined to bed in a hospital near you. What would you be doing if that was a member of your family in the hospital?

Why not arrange to visit a few hospital-bound children. Take them a treat (check with the nurses to see what's permissible!). Take a favorite board game and play it with them. Read stories from an inspiring book. Or just sit and talk. Your company may be the very best gift you can give them.

Organizing Games for the Community

Organize a softball game (or soccer, or basketball) for the kids of your neighborhood. Pick up the players, or better yet invite their parents to come and observe.

Keep the game friendly – lots of umpires or referees help. And collect donations to provide hot dogs, popcorn and soda. Sit down on the field after the game and ask what else you can do to keep these games happening and keep them fun.

Design Your Own Thank You Cards

Design and create a box of thank you cards. Use your own illustrations, pictures you cut out of art magazines or fabric remnants. Sign your name on the back of the cards.

Use the cards to correspond with people who have done something you appreciate. Or give the cards as a gift to someone you know who writes a lot of letters.

Going to the Grocery Store

Go to the grocery store for someone who is sick or recovering at home, or for someone for whom it is getting more and more difficult to get out of the house.

Meet with the individual ahead of time. Create a shopping list together. Be sure to ask about preferred brand names, sizes and flavors. Return with the groceries and the receipt. Throw in a surprise bonus or two from your family.

Cheering Up a Nearby Family

Talk to your pastor or principal to locate a family who needs some extra cheering up. Make an initial visit to ascertain what you could do for the family. Then visit again with a new flower box, a ready-to-eat meal, an evening of fun and games, or a Bible study on a topic that would be encouraging.

Keep in touch with the family. Be sure to invite them to join you in church.

Volunteer Agencies Need You

Volunteer to work at a community agency that performs regular service for the people of your town. Look into the personnel needed by animal shelters, day care centers, head start programs, hostile services, even youth ministry resource centers.

Welcome to Our Neighborhood

Develop a community map that would be useful to new members of your community. Include on the map the location of places such as the post office, libraries, shopping malls, grocery stores, banks, restaurants, and churches. Don't forget services like dry cleaners, shoe repair, florists, hospitals and clinics. Also include the phone numbers for utility companies, police and fire departments. You may also want to recommend day care centers or baby-sitting services.

When people move into your community, visit them with a fresh loaf of bread, homemade cookies or one of your special pies. Then give them the community map with best wishes for their new home.

Additional Activities to Help Encourage a Life of Service

On these pages, record activities which your family creates to help encourage a life of service in your home.

_____

_____

_____

_____

_____

_____

_____

_____

_____

_____

_____

_____

_____

_____

_____

_____

_____

_____

_____

_____

_____

_____

The Colors of Grace in Our Homes

Index of Bible Passages

The Old Testament

The New Testament

Index of Activity
Skills and Interests

Activities for Everyone in the Family

In the creation of this little book of practical suggestions, we've tried to include activities that will involve all the members of the family, regardless of their interests, gifts, skills or talents.

Consequently, you'll find projects for people who like to work with their hands, people who are artistic and creative, people who are primarily verbal, people who do behind-the-scenes organizing better than they do up-front presentations, people who have the gift of prayer, people who like to act, people who enjoy cooking, and people who prefer working with computers.

The following index divides the book's activities into these areas of gifts, skills, talents, and interests. If someone in your home needs encouragement in one of these areas, begin with those projects that will involve that individual and move to projects that will develop additional skills.

Art

Bible Study

Comparing

Computers

Cooking

The Colors of Grace in Our Homes

Creative Writing

Drama

Film, TV, and Video

Research

Things to Do Outside

Things to Do With Your Hands

Valuing